Stock Market Investing for Beginners

Gary Jenks

Published by The Heirs Publishing Company, 2019.

STOCK MARKET INVESTING FOR BEGINNERS

First edition. July 17, 2019.

Copyright © 2019 Gary Jenks.

ISBN: 978-1393597520

Written by Gary Jenks.

Stock Market Investing for Beginners
Your Guide to Long-Term Financial Freedom
Through Trading
By: Gary Jenks and Benjamin Ramsey

Introduction

This book was created as a complete beginner's guide to investing in stock, and it provides adequate short chapters with in-depth knowledge where you can take your time and study to know more about investing in stocks.

Just like new investors, you concluded on investing in a business and then pick up the first dividends of the stock, but since you have very little knowledge about it, you keep deliberating on your plan. Do not worry about that as this book will help you understand how to invest in stocks. To be more specific about this, it will help new investors. This was collated to help introduce a depository of other investment topics necessary to know the basics known as I guide you through your journey in stock market investing.

Four Key Ways to Invest in Stocks

Here are four key ways to invest in stocks:

1. Invest through a stock broker account
2. Invest through a traditional IRA account
3. Invest through a 401k plan or 403b plan (for a non-profit account)
4. Invest through a Dividend reinvestment or Direct stock acquisition plan

Five Assets from Stock Investment

There are five types of asset in which the average investor is likely to possess in his/her lifetime, whether or not that person did not invest in the asset directly or through a pooled structure such as index funds, exchange-traded funds, hedge fund, or mutual fund.

1. **Preferred stocks:** This is a unique type of stock that often pays greater dividends but has its limited upside.
2. **Real Estate Investment Trust (REITs):** This is an exceptional type of company's allotment that gives way to no taxation at the company's level provided that 90% of the earnings are to be paid to shareholders; these assets are usually invested in real estate properties and projects.
3. **Common stocks:** Once you invest in stocks, you will possess an ownership share in a business operating stake along with a share of the disposable earnings and the dividends that are made by the firm. Though you do not have to invest in stocks to become wealthy, over the past few centuries, stocks have been the highest returning class asset and have produced more wealth.
4. **Bonds:** When you lend money to either a municipality, business, country, or every other institution, you are buying bonds like municipal bonds, savings bonds, corporate bonds, U.S government Treasury bonds, etc.
5. **Money markets:** They are highly fluid investments that are required to protect your purchasing power; they are considered a cash equivalent. There are two types: money market funds and money market accounts. There are also five other alternatives to money markets.

Why You Need to Research When Investing in Stocks

When you are researching an investment, there are five basic documents that you will need to get your hands on to ascertain the merit of the productive stock. The documents which you should have been easy to find. They are:

- Statistics showing 5-10 years back. Different companies provide this information in a straightforward format mostly for a small fee. Some research products or houses like the Valueline investment survey, Morningstar, Moody's, and the Standard & Poor's.
- The most recent form 10-Q: This is a quarterly variation of the form 10-K
- Proxy Statement: This includes information on the Board of directors as well as the shareholder's proposal and management compensation.
- Recent annual report: While you are going through the annual report, you will pay attention to the letter from the chairman, sometimes CFO, CEO, or other high-ranking officers to know how well they view the business. Note that not all annual reports are created equal, and the best in the business is known to be the one written by Warren Buffet at Berkshire Hathaway which is available to download free on the company's holding site.
- The form 10-K: This is the annual filing of the Securities and Exchange Commission (SEC), and this is probably the single-most important research document available to investors about the company.

Three Financial Statements Necessary for Stock Investing

It is vital that you look deeply into the financial statements before buying an ownership stake by investing in the company's stock:

1. The balance sheet
2. The cash flow statement
3. The income statement

All these three financial statements can reinforce and work together in which you cannot decide to study them in isolation or try to make decisions based on limited data; a mistake that can be much more costly particularly when you choose to invest in stock rather than a senior security that is higher in their capital structures such as a bond.

This book explains the nitty-gritty of the stock market to beginners interested in venturing into the profitable world of the stock market. With the facts, strategies, and experiences shared, you will be armed with sufficient information to make the right investment decision. As a beginner, your first step to making a wise financial investment in the stock market begins by reading this book.

In the ensuing chapters of this book, I will be discussing all you need to know about the stock market as a viable tool for investment and making money.

I look forward to you taking full control of your financial future after reading this book.

Happy reading!

Chapter 1 : How Stocks Work

The stock market boasts of an excellent history in this modern era as an efficient and effective means of boosting capital, wealth, and passive income. Despite the importance of stock trading, most people, including investors, often misunderstand its purpose. A vast majority of the population views the stock market as an area that defies explanation; a series of random numbers and letters that vary from time to time without reason.

However, a well-chosen stock is capable of providing financial freedom and flexibility to follow your passions. Here are the things to know about stock market investing.

What Is Stock?

Simply put, owning stock signifies legal ownership in a business. Two types of stock are often issued by corporations, namely: common stocks and preferred stocks. Another name for a stock is "securities," as they provide financial security.

Common Stocks

These are the most common stocks available to anyone planning to invest in the stock — common stockholder shares in the proportionate profit or losses of the company. The stockholders are responsible for electing the company's Board of Directors and can also hire and fire the CEO. The CEO and Board of Directors decide whether to keep the profits made or release some or all earnings as cash dividend to the stockholder. A cash dividend refers to a check or electronic transfer forwarded to the brokerage or retirement account holding the stock.

Preferred Stocks

A specific dividend is received at predetermined times by shareholders of this type of stock. Typically, the dividend of preferred stock is paid first before that of the common stockholder. Unlike the common stockholder, who shares in the business profit and loss, the preferred stockholder is exempted in the case of bankruptcy.

Why Does Stock Exist?

There are several reasons why stocks exist, chief amongst them are the following:

- Stocks provide companies with the means of achieving capitalization for their business growth. Market capitalization has been one of the most innovative ways to drive business growth, all thanks to the stock market.
- Stocks give investors the perfect opportunity to earn returns on capital investment that may be more rewarding than if they had ventured into other business.
- Stocks allow investors who have no interest in management to participate through voting rights which brings about a balanced allocation of resources.

Practical Example of How Stocks Work

Here is a practical example of how stock works so that you will get a better understanding of the stock market.

Let's imagine you intend to start a family-owned retail store. In your financial plan, you discovered you need $200,000 to start up the business, so you decide to incorporate a new company.

You divide the company into stock shares of 2,000 with each new share priced $100. Imagine selling all the shares needed for the business capital to your family members; you would realize the $200,000 needed for the business startup (2000 shares x $100 per capital share = $200,000 cash generated for the business).

In the first financial year, if the retail store made $50,000 profit after tax, then each stock share would be given.

If the store earned $50,000 after taxes during its first year, each share of stock would qualify to receive 1/2, 000th of the profit. $50,000 will be divided by 2,000, resulting in $40 EPS (earnings per share). You could also hold a meeting with the Board of Directors to deliberate on what to do with the money, to pay as dividends, repurchase some stock, or reinvest in the company.

In the course of the business, you may choose to sell your shares of the family store. You could consider an IPO (initial public offering) for large businesses which would enable you to sell your stock on a stock exchange market.

Often, this is what plays out when you purchase or sell company shares through a stockbroker. You are signifying an interest in buying or selling a certain company's shares. Wall Street then links you with someone willing to either buy or sell, and they receive their fees and commissions from the transaction.

On the other hand, stock shares could be issued to raise several millions of dollars for expansion. For example, Sam Walton the founder of Wal-Mart Stores, Inc., raise an IPO that enabled him to sell new shares of stock where he raised enough cash to pay off most of his debt and reinvest in Wal-Mart's expansion.

How Does an Investor Make Profit From Owning Stocks?

Ideally, there are three ways to make a profit from investments as a passive stockholder under normal circumstances. Firstly, you can receive cash dividends sent to you as your share of profit from the company. Secondly, you can benefit from an increase in your share value. Thirdly, you can make a profit from valuation change related to the company's earnings or other assets. These three ways of making a profit make up what we term as an investment's total return.

Deciding Stocks Worth Owning

Deciding on the ideal stock to own depends on many factors. Most beginners or novices in stock market investment think that their main objective is to maximize profit; this is an erroneous belief as owning stock goes beyond that.

In some cases, it could be a way to get satisfactory returns with minimal risk or it could be a way of increasing cash flow by concentrating on high yielding securities such as blue-chip stocks with high dividends.

Below are some characteristics to look for when considering the stock to invest in:

- Businesses with a track record of sustained or increasing profitability in the course of an entire business cycle including at least one period of recession.
- Businesses that are friendly to their shareholders,and whose Board of Directors are keen to remit excess capital to shareholders through increasing dividends and share repurchases.
- Businesses with high returns on investments (ROI).
- Businesses with a strong competitive presence and advantage over other competitors.

After choosing the business stock based on these characteristics, you would then analyze how each stock fits together as part of an investment portfolio. Ideally, you should diversify your investments into several businesses to offset issues like correlated risk.

What Is the Main Aim of Investing in Stocks?

Astute investors know that the ultimate goal for most stock owners is to end up with a pool of brilliant businesses that generate lots of cash they can use to live a fulfilled life. I believe that making enormous investments in stocks should be a long-term appreciation of shares rather than buying at one price and quickly selling it off for profit. It's a stock you could leave for over 25 years and watch how its value keeps rising within this period even though the stock price itself is volatile.

That is indeed the story about how some made their fortune, like Anne Scheiber, a retired IRS agent who accumulated tens of millions from her apartment by using her spare time to study and analyze stocks, which she invested in for decades. Janitor Ronald Read and Jack MacDonald made a fortune of $8 million and $188 million respectively from stock market trading. Several other examples abound of secret millionaires who have made a vast wealth from the stock market. It wasn't a case of luck; instead, it is a case of those who dedicated their free time to research business shares they want to invest in.

Another thing to note about these successful people is that they never ventured into these investments with the aim of getting rich overnight. The shares of different companies were bought and locked away while they focused on other things without putting all their investments in a single enterprise. The stock market is a long-term investment with the potential of multiplying your initial capital several times, so make the wise decision today.

Chapter 2: How to Invest in Stocks

To grow more wealth, the best way to do that is to invest in stocks. But how exactly is this done? Follow the necessary steps and learn how to invest in the stock market.

1. Select the Investing style

Different ways are used to approach investing stocks. Choose an option below that best represents the situation:

- "I know stocks can be an excellent investment, but I will need someone to help me manage the process for me." For a Robo-advisor, you might be a perfect candidate for a service that provides low-cost investment management. Mostly, all stockbrokers have this service available today; they help you invest your money based on your specific vision or goals. Check out the top picks for Robo-advisors, and once you find the choice that you prefer, then you are ready to shop for an account.
- "I am the DIY type, am interested in choosing stocks and stock funds for myself." When you keep feeding yourself more information, this book will tell you everything that you will need to know or, if you are already aware of the stock-buying game and all you need is a brokerage, check for some of the best online stock brokers.

2. Open an Account

Speaking generally, to invest in stock, you will need an investment account. For the hands-on type, this is sometimes referred to as a brokerage account. If you want a little help, Robo-advisor will be the best option to use. There is an analysis of the process below:

The 401k option

This is a type of investment account, and if you are already in one, you might be investing in stocks through mutual funds. Though a 401k stock might not give you straight access to individual stocks and choice in mutual funds might be quite limited. The employer matching dollar makes it worthwhile with their contributions, despite a limited investment selection, but once you have contributed so well to earn it, then you can consider investing in other accounts.

The DIY option: Opening a Brokerage account

Online brokerage accounts likely offer you the least expensive and quickest methods of buying funds, stock, and varieties of other investment. With a broker, it is possible to open an individual retirement account which is also known as IRA. There are also top picks for IRA accounts, or you can open a taxable brokerage account when you are confident that you are saving well for your retirement somewhere else.

There is a 3 step guide for opening a brokerage account if you need to dive deep. You will need to assess brokers based on factors like cost (account fees, trading commission), selections for investment (looking for a good selection commission – free ETS if you favor funds), tools, and investor research.

There are two reliable options of the best online stock brokers; they are Merrill Edge (they are the top pick for research that has no account minimum) and Ally Invest

(top pick for low-cost category).

3. Distinguish Between Stocks and Stock Mutual Funds

Are you going the DIY route? Do not be bothered as a stock investment does not have to be complicated. For a lot of people, stock investment has to do with these two types of investment:

Equity

Equity is also known as stock mutual funds or exchange-traded funds. These mutual funds allow you to purchase a small piece of many different stocks in just a single transaction. ETF'S and Index funds are mutual funds that can track an index; for example, Standard & Poor's 500 funds can copy the index by buying stocks from the companies. When you can invest in funds like this, you also own a piece of that company. You can also gather several other funds to put together a diversified range of products.

Individual Stocks

If you are after a particular type of company, it is possible to buy a single share or few shares to have in stock – trading waters. Put together a portfolio that is diversified out of several individual stocks available, but this takes significant investment.

The upside of stock investment is that they are unavoidably diversified which allows for less risk, and they are unlikely to rise brilliantly as some individual stock might. Upside stocks individually are that someone who is wise can pick, and it will pay off handsomely, but there are odds that any individual stock can make you wealthy are very rare or slim. For a large number of investors, especially for those who are investing in their retirement, builds their portfolio which includes mutual funds as their choice.

4. Set a Budget

Upcoming investors have two questions in this process:

1. How much should I invest in stocks?

If you are going to invest through funds as I mentioned earlier, you can set aside a large portion of the portfolio to stock funds especially when you are looking at a long-term horizon. An investment of 30 years for retirement can yield an 80% of his/her portfolio in stock funds, and the rest will be put into bond funds. Another story entirely is the individual stock; I would recommend that you keep 10% or less for investment portfolio.

1. How much do I need to start investing in stocks?

The amount of money that you need depends on how expensive the shares are (the price generally ranges from a few dollars to thousands of dollars). If you want to have a mutual fund and the money you have is not sufficient then an ETF (Exchange-traded funds) will be the best option. Mutual funds usually have a minimum of $1000 or less.

5. Start Investing

This type of stock investment has more complexity strategically and in approaches, yet some of the most successful ones have done much more than sticking to the basics of it. This also means using funds for the size of your portfolio. Warren Buffet famously said that a low cost of about $500 index funds is one of the best investments that most Americans can make. Choose individual stock when you believe that the company has the capacity to grow over an extended period.

Should You Invest in Stock or Mutual Funds?

This is a question that needs an honest answer. I will say that when you invest in stocks, you are not buying from a share of a particular company but from a mutual fund; it permits more diversification by bonding with many company stocks and putting it together as an investment. Stocks should consist more of bulk portfolios geared towards a goal that is set for the long-term, for example, retirement. It doesn't mean that you will not buy and also trade individual stocks; you can also acquire knowledge through equity mutual funds.

Mutual Stocks vs. Stocks

Stocks are investments in a single company while mutual funds have many other investments which mean that they have up to hundreds of stocks in just a single fund. You can read through the strategy below, but we will give more information for those who want to know more. We also recommend that investors own a large portion of their portfolio with mutual funds (especially low-cost index and exchange-traded funds which is also referred to as ETF). Once you are set, you can also give time to set apart 5% or 10% of your portfolio to get stocks trading for a little pleasure.

Mutual Funds
Cons

- Can be less tax-efficient
- Annual expense ratios
- Trade only once a day after the market closes but ETF trades are on an exchange like stocks
- Funds have investments up to %1,000 or more

Pros

- Many index funds and ETF's have low ongoing fees
- Easy diversifications as each fund owns small pieces of many other investments
- Convenient and less time intensive for the investor
- Professional management available through actively managed funds.

Explanation
Equity mutual funds act just like intermediaries between stocks and you. They gather the investor's money and divert it into different

other companies. Rather than selecting or picking an individual stock to form a portfolio, it is possible for you to buy many other stocks in just one transaction through mutual funds. This makes mutual funds perfect for investors who do not want to spend their time managing a portfolio of individual stocks in which a mutual fund will work out for you. An investment portfolio might contain as few as two mutual funds.

The key to mutual funds is that there are different types of mutual funds, namely:

- Actively managed funds. They are controlled by a professional manager.
- Index funds. They can track benchmark index like the Standard & Poor's $500
- ETF's which are all under the category of the index which typically tracks an index but they are traded all day like stocks.

I am a big fan of ETF's and index funds that are actively managed mutual funds and here is the reason: while most professional managers try to beat the market, most times they do not, immediately you tried to adjust the fee. And as you know, any funds that take the service of a professional manager come with a higher fee. Tracking benchmarks with either ETF's or index funds give an excellent shot at returns from short-term investment, along with lower fees and diversification.

Bear in mind that mutual funds are not entirely hands-off: You will still have to stay on top of your portfolio, which you will need to rebalance from time to time, check the fees, and make sure that you are still invested at the suitable level of risk. If you do want just that, it might be a good option for you to use Robo-advisor, portfolio management services that are online invested for their clients, and rebalance the portfolio as needed. These types of companies invest in ETF's.

Individual Stocks

Cons

- You will have to pay a commission to buy or sell
- It is time intensive, as investors must duly research and follow each stock in their portfolio
- Has more risks than mutual funds
- Most hold many individual shares to diversify adequately

Pros

- No ongoing or annual fees
- Tax efficient, as it is possible to control capital gains by timing when you buy or sell
- Highly liquid
- Total control over companies in which you choose to invest

Explanation

Can you do most of the work of ETF's, index funds, or mutual funds all by yourself, by getting stocks outright? That's if you are ready to quit working and start trading. This is really an ambitious and time-consuming effort to build portfolios from individual stocks. Each of these stocks require good findings; you will have to dig deep into the company you are trying to invest in, as well as its financial and quarterly reports, industry and management (there are ways to research). You will need to put together a number of these individual stocks into portfolios that manage risk by diversifying into companies or industry size and geographical region.

Some investors love to invest in stocks and mutual funds, should investing become pleasurable. Being bored is also cool. But when you want to select one that works best for you, why not try compromising: by setting aside a little portion of funds for active stock trading while you try to invest the remaining in a diversified portfolio of ETF's and index funds.

Chapter 3: Why Stocks Fluctuate

Ask different people about stocks and one major thing I know everyone agrees on is that the prices of stocks vary irregularly. They either increase or decrease in value at times with shocking amounts in a single trading day.

Why do prices fluctuate? Who or what causes fluctuation?

These are questions that are usually asked by beginners in stock investment. To further expatiate on this, I will give an overview of some of the things that cause stock to be unpredictable. Some of this may look technical to you but at the end of this chapter, you will be more versatile than the general public about how stocks operate and how stock prices are being set.

The Stock Market Is an Auction

Realize one thing: the stock market is an auction, with a party willing to sell its ownership and another party trying to buy its ownership when they have been able to agree a standard price then the trade is suitable and becomes what the market quotation is. The buyers and sellers can be corporations, governments, individuals, or asset management companies that help the private client manage their money, index funds, pension plans, or mutual funds. In so many cases, you might not have an idea who is trading on the other side.

Due to the fact that the stock market functions like an auction, where there are more buyers than sellers, this actually makes rates increase, thereby increasing the quotations of the market at which the investors can also sell their shares, attracting investors who do not want to sell their shares to become suddenly interested and want to share. However, when there are more sellers than buyers, there is a rush to sell to the lowest bidder and then set the prices in a race to the least.

This can actually become a problem especially during the collapse period of 2007-2009 because institutions such as Lehman Brothers had no choice but to dump everything they could just to raise funds. This overwhelmed the market with a tradeable financial asset that has more worth to a long-term buyer than the price at which the brothers were willing to sell.

What Influences Buyer and Seller

On a typical day, values of stock do not move much, but you will see the value rising and falling at a percentage of one or two points with large swings occasionally. Most days, investors make a purchasing decision based on an assessment of the balance sheet of that particular company and the total impression of whether the company's price is fair or not. There are times when events occur that cause the price to either rise or fall quickly. This could be the earnings report that shows the good or bad financial news, and it could also be major financial news such as an increase in the interest rate. It could be a natural disaster such as a hurricane.

In a few cases, the stock price fluctuates because a requisite of money flow percentage in the market at a particular time is not taking a long-term enterprise. The illustration used was the equity valuation given to a known jeweler, Tiffany & company. The long-term value of the firm totally undeserved the unpredictable share of Tiffany price years back when the article was written. First of all, hedge funds hiked the price far beyond what any buyer wanted to pay, and when it was like the world was struggling for it, dumped it and drove down beyond what the same set of people might want to pay.

As a novice in stock trading, you should understand that it's normal for stocks to fluctuate and these unpredictable ways can cause the journey to be rough. This necessitates the need to diversify the portfolio and focus on look-through earnings.

Chapter 4: How to Manage Overvalued and Undervalued Stock

How to Know an Overvalued Stock

Different investors are always asking this question of how they can figure it out, if and when stocks are overvalued. The price-to-earnings ratio offers a quick method to estimate the company's value, but it will not mean much until you understand how to explain the result. A stock is assigned as overvalued when the current price is not supported by its earnings projections or price-to-earnings, which is also known as earnings multiple. If the price of the company's stock is 50 times earnings, for example, this is likely to be overvalued compared to 10 times the earnings of other companies.

Though there are some investors who still think the stock market is effectual and an average investor might not have the desired information that will be enough to know overpriced stocks because it is immediately included into stock prices, analysts believe that you will always find either undervalued or overvalued shares in the market due to irrational behaviors of investors.

How is it possible to know if a share is overpriced?

Different signals can be useful which eventually indicates a closer look is guaranteed. It is important to start surveying the company's annual report, income statement, balance sheet, 10-K filing, and every other disclosure to know more about the firm's operation using pieces of information that can be accessed easily. Though many investors depend on the price-to-earnings ratio, if you are trying to dig much more effectively, there are other ways to test if a stock is overvalued. Some of the indicators of overvalued stock are mentioned below:

Check the PEG or Dividend-Adjusted PEG Ratio

These two different calculations can be useful in almost all situations, but they also have the rare exception that comes out from time to time. The first thing to consider is the after-tax project growth in earnings per share within a couple of years ago, fully diluted. Then, look at the price-to-earnings ratio of the stock, using the two figures; it is possible to calculate something which is called the PEG ratio using this formula:

PEG ratio= P/E/Company's earnings growth rate.

If the stocks pay a dividend, then you may want to use the dividend-adjusted PEG ratio formula:

Dividend-adjusted PEG ratio= P/E/ (earnings growth + dividend yield)

The upper absolute threshold that everyone considers is a ratio of 2. Using this case, the lower the number, the better it is. Anything that is 1 or below is considered a very good deal. Another thing is that there are exceptions. For example, an investor with lots of industry knowledge might experience a turnaround in a recurring business and know if the earnings projections are too conservative. Though some situations can appear to be rosier at the beginning for new investors, this general rule might protect against preventable loss.

Check the Relative Dividend Revenue Percentage

You might discover that an overvalued stock dividend has in the lowest 20% yield of its long-term historical range except for the industry, sector, business is going through a thorough change. Either the economic forces are at work or in its business model; a company's essential operations leads to exhibit of some amount of stability over a period of time with a fair, realistic range of results under certain conditions.

That is, the stock market could be variable, but the real functioning experience of most businesses during major periods shows it as being stable; at least they are measured over the total economic cycles shown in the stock value and this can be used to the advantage of the investor. Take a company like Chevron. Looking at the previous years, all through history, any time the dividend of Chevron gets lower than 2.00%, investors have to be very careful as the firm is being overvalued. Also, any time it reaches 3.50% to a 4.00% range, it takes another look as it is being undervalued.

The yield of the dividend serves as a signal; it is one of the ways that inexperienced investors estimate the relative price to the business profits, strip off lots of difficulties that can come up whenever you are dealing with financial information under standards like GAAP. To check and track the company's dividend over a certain period, draw out the past dividends over other days and then divide the chart equally into five distributions. Any time the dividends fall lower than the quintile bottom be cautious.

As with every other method, this one is also not perfect. Successful companies also run into trouble suddenly and fall. Bad businesses can also have a turnaround and then increase suddenly. On average, when a conservative investor follows it as part of the high-quality well-run portfolios, dividend-paying stocks, blue-chips, this method of approach also generates outstanding results which can also make investors behave mechanically.

Study the Prospect of a Cyclical Industry

There are few companies like automobile manufacturers, home builders, and so on that possess certain unique characteristics. These companies tend to experience sharp drops in profit during an economic recession, and they experience an increase during the time of economic expansion. When the time of economic expansion occurs, investors are attracted by what looks like a fast-growing earning, low profit-to-earnings and also, in some other cases, large dividends. These situations which are referred to as value ruses can be deadly as they look like the end of the economic surplus cycles which can trap less experienced investors. Grounded investors are always aware that, in reality, the ratio of price-to-earnings of these companies is much greater than what is visible.

Check the Yield

Stock earning yield compared to the Treasury bond revenue can also provide ways to test an overestimated stock. Whenever the Treasury bonds are over the earning yields by a ratio of 3:1, it is not encouraging to go in. Calculate this through the following formula:

(30-year Treasury bond revenue/2) Fully-diluted revenue per share

For instance, if a business earns $1.00 per share in a diluted EPS and 30-year treasury bond revenue is 5.00%, this stock will test to show it is overvalued if you paid $40.00 or more per share. This sends a red flag that you return adopted extraordinary optimism. Treasury bond yield exceeds earning by 3:1 has only occurred a few times every ten years or more, but that is never good. If it is occurring in so many stocks, the stock market will have excessive high relative to Gross National Product (GNP), which is one of the major caution signs that it is detached from the valuations from the underlying economic reality.

Never forget to modify for financial cycles, though. For example, in the 2001 September 11th economic meltdown, lots of businesses had significant write-offs that led to severe depressing incomes and extremely high price-to-earnings ratios. The enterprise was able to stand in the years following that since there was no indefinite damage done to the core operations in almost all cases.

Overpriced Shares in Your Portfolio

It is necessary for every investor to know the difference between rejecting to buy overvalued stocks and also not selling such stocks. There are enough reasons why many smart investors may not want to sell an overpriced stock that is in their portfolio, many of which include trade-off decisions about tax regulations and opportunity cost. After that has been said, it is better to hold on to something that might have 25% higher than the conservative approximate inherent value, and another total which is if you are holding stocks with values so overestimated it makes no sense even in a normal market.

One of the dangers with new investors is the way they can often trade when you own stocks in very good business which will likely increase the return on equity, high return on working capital, high return on assets, and the inherent stock value is likely to increase over time. It is often a blunder to part with a company's share just because it has increased from time to time. Take a look at the yields of these two companies, PepsiCo and Coca-Cola. Even when the stock prices are overvalued, an investor might regret selling off his/her stake.

How to Know an Undervalued Stock?

An undervalued stock is one that sells lower than its inherent value, Wikipedia refers to intrinsic value as the value of a company's currency, product, or stock, determined through analysis without any reference to its market value. It is also referred to as Fundamental Value which can be gotten by calculating or analyzing the return on capital management, cash flow, profit retention, and return asset through the company's financial assessment. You need to have a thorough grasp of how to identify an undervalued stock and how to make it work for you regardless of its value.

Why and When Is Stock Undervalued?

There are different points why a stock can sometimes be undervalued; two or more situations can be played at the same time. They include:

Herd Mentality

So many people invest in the market momentum, and they follow what other investors do. During a rise in the company's market or if the stock price of the company increases, investors will want to buy. This behavior is fueled partially by the fact they believe they might have missed out, like their desire to get into the game. All they want is to position themselves to future benefits by buying stocks that will be trading above the inherent value just for them to feel "in the know."

This also applies to stocks when they are falling or when the market is set to decline, and investors then begin to fear that they might lose all and by that they rush to sell, instead of waiting for the prices to go back up as it surely will. They would prefer to sell their stocks at a lower price. This behavior is so bad that it can increase in a downward manner in the market.

Bad Press

Bad press details a company's setbacks, resulting in their stock price reducing. The effect does not make sense just because all the companies have obstacles that must be subdued. A single litigious or recall event does not generally mean that the company is downward or no longer has any value.

Cyclic Behavior

Many businesses go through the cycles of increase and reduced profits; this can be due to something mild at the time of the year. For instance, a company in the lawn equipment sector is surely going to see fewer profits during winter and will see higher profits in the summer.

Non-trendy Stocks

We know that all stocks have a status attached to them, especially the ones you must own. Especially the common stock that is well established in the industry. If you are taking questionnaires and asking investors if they would rather invest in Johnson & Johnson or Google, almost everyone will choose Google, not just because Google is a leader in the technology sector that is trending, but because it is in the news far more than Johnson & Johnson which makes consumer goods.

Market Bubbles and Crashes

When, as an investor, you tap into the market momentum and herd mentality; panic can set in and ensure that it might cause a crash. The 1929 Wall Street crash that sparked depression is a blooming example. This kind of attitude can also increase stock market bubbles where over-investment makes the stock price so high that the fundamentals cannot support the price. Then, the stock crashes.

Quiet Stocks

A stock that stays on the radar because it is not known or because it is not trending in the news can easily become undervalued. Small caps and foreign stocks are an example of stocks that go unnoticed by most investors.

Finding Undervalued Stocks

Finding undervalued stocks with time is likely going to sift through other companies, their financial reports. The official website contains the information needed to make a qualified decision. Compiling data can also be used to track results and narrow down the stocks you are to invest in. It is very important just for you to stay focused and organized.

Making Undervalued Stocks Work for You

One of the strategies for the value-based investment is to find stocks that are undervalued and buy them when the prices are lower than the original company's values. Investors following a value duly in investing strategy think the market will likely improve, and the share price will increase as it overcomes the challenges faced. Another strategy is to avoid stocks that might be overvalued by the market to protect the portfolio from the risk of possible downside overvalued holdings.

Whether a stock is overvalued or undervalued, you need to pay attention to the above details before making your next financial decision. The decision you make might be the one single decision that will usher in a windfall of multi-million dollars and financial stability.

Chapter 5: Valuing Stocks

The prices of stock changes with time (sometimes it can be a within a minute) which is as a result of market forces. This means that the value of shares increase due to fluctuation in demand and supply. If many people want to buy a stock at a given time (demand) and then sell it (supply), then it is normal for the prices to move up.

Conversely, if people are enthusiastic about selling stock rather than buying it, there will be more supply than demand, and then the prices will eventually fall. Certainly, for any trade to occur there has to be both the buyer and the seller available in which the number of the buyers and sellers is the same. Here I mean the number of enthusiastic buyers or sellers, i.e., those willing to buy at a more costly price or sell at a low rate.

The price of the stock shows the "value" of the corporation, at its basic level. The price is calculated by dividing the dollar value of that company which is referred to as the market capitalization (or market cap) outstanding by the number of shares. For example, if a Corp is estimated at $1,000,000 and it has $100,000 shares, the share price for a single share will be $10.00. Conversely, one can also know the company's market value by just multiplying the share price by the amount of shares. The question that pops up is: what causes fluctuation in the company's value?

What Does a Company's Value Represent?

A company has and sells pieces of stuff. The items it has includes documents, money in the bank, machinery, buildings, etc. which constitute its book value, or the amount of money that a company will possess if they sold everything they have at once. A company's primary goal is to make profits and to achieve that is by selling either their product or their services. The total value of the company depends basically on the stuff it has and the cash flow that will come in future. The worth of the stuff it owns is easy to comprehend but the value of the expected cash flow can be a bit tricky, and this is the cause of a market revolution.

Expected future profits must be reduced to represent the present day dollar value due to the time value of money — the dollar that is kept in a bank today is worth much more in the future after it has earned more interest, but in reverse.

The amount of reduction in cash flow in the future basically depends on lots of things which includes the cost of capital (which is the cost to either fund or borrow investment, which totally depends on interest rate), the risk of the business (in stock market this is often approximated using beta) with the restrain cost of absolutely doing nothing and also saving your money in the bank (risk-free rate or opportunity cost).

Once the appropriately reduced rate has been approximated, then the difficult part is to figure out what the future cash flow will be like from a year from now, a month from now, or even five years from now. Expectations and sentiment are large makeup parts of these predictions and also analysis financially to distinguish the amount accountable for both macro factors and company-specific factors like overall economic health.

Luckily, the stock market follows the expectations of future cash flow in a very easy way to calculate the ratio for price-to-earnings which is also referred to as the P/E ratio. A price-to-earnings ratio of about 10X means that the company's values are 10x the current earning of the company. A P/E ratio of 20X for the same company also means that it will give the same amount of earnings. The market is giving twice as much value which indicates that the future cash flow will be higher. Of course, there are also some appealing price models that analysts can use rather than the P/E ratio, like the free cash flow models or dividend discount models.

Since the future is mostly unknown in our world today, stock values will differ from one another, giving some a lesser stock price while giving others an increase in normal stock prices. If the price is lower than the expected price, then people will buy it. When the economy is getting better, people spend, and profits are also rising; companies begin to invest in projects, they expand their businesses and employ more people. Investors are optimistic, and they have expectations of future cash flow increase, and then stocks enter a bull market.

Also, stock prices can decrease when the expectations of future cash flow decrease, making the prices of the companies seem to increase greatly; therefore, it causes people to sell their shares. If there are lots of people that take this decision than the people who are willing to buy the shares, the price will continue to fall until it gets to a level where people will begin to believe that they are not valued.

The important things to note about these complicated subjects are as follows:

• Price multiplied by the outstanding shares (market capitalization) gives the value of the company which compares the share price of the two companies is meaningless.

• There are so many competing theories that will try to give details about the way the stock prices move the way they do. Unfortunately, there is no theory to explain everything.

• At the most fundamental level, the demand and supply in the market determines stock prices at any given moment.

• Theoretically, earnings are what affect an investor's valuation of a company, but there are other indicators that investors use to predict stock prices. It is the investors' attitudes, expectations, and sentiments that ultimately affect the stock prices whether they rise or fall.

The importance of knowing stock value before investing in shares cannot be overemphasized. Therefore, you should do an in-depth study of the company you wish before you invest in their stock.

Chapter 6 : Bulls, Bears and Market Sentiment

Investors usually have various beliefs about a specific stock or how the economy will be directed as a whole. Every day in trading seems parallel to strife between the pessimists and also the optimists who sell and buy at different prices with various expectations. The stock market is said to possess all necessary pieces of information about the companies it constitutes in which the price also manifests. Whenever the optimists tend to rule the market, the prices of stocks tend to increase, and then we conclude we are in a **Bull market,** but when the opposite becomes a reality, the prices of stocks tend to decrease, then we are in a **Bear market**.

A bull market tells us that everything in the economy is running indisputably fine when people can get jobs, and then the rate of unemployment reduces, the gross domestic product measures how the economy is doing well, and stocks increasing. During the time things are going smoothly, it is very easy to decide to pick a stock. If a person who is optimistic decides that stocks will increase, that person is referred to as a Bull and is known to have an outlook of a bull. Sometimes, we all know that the bull market cannot remain like this forever and this might lead to deadly situations when stocks are becoming overvalued.

One of the negative ways of the bull market is also referred to as **Bubble**, where the increased target of the stock prices no longer behaves like the fundamentals and sentiment from the optimistic takeover. Over the years, bubbles consistently occurred dating back to the time of the Dutch Tulipmania of the 1600s in which the prices on tulip increased so much that one could be worth the same as a house, and this made the great recession occur through the housing bubble. Bubbles usually occur when the truth catches us with over hiked prices, and then people realize that bubbles are nothing but the nature of events. It is very hard to know when investors are in the time of a bubble, and it will be much more difficult to know when it is going to pop up.

Bear markets are usually defined irregularly broad indices that drop 20%; this primarily occurs when the economy is in a time of recession when corporate profits fall. There is unemployment and GDP contracts. Bear markets make it very tough for almost all investors to select a profitable stock and one of the best solutions to this is profit from the time the stocks are falling through what is called short selling. Another form is to wait significantly from the sidelines until you observe that the bear market is almost over, and you begin to buy again.

Bear markets are expected to be associated with the rise in the unpredictability of the stock market since most investors have a phobia for losses much more than they accumulate gains at a level, which is emotional. Most people are not just rational actors particularly when it comes to their investment and money. At the time of the bear market, prices do not reduce systematically or logically of price-to-earnings at a fundamental level but usually, those who participate in the market overreact in fear and then give prices at a low valuation which are still reasonable.

Whenever there is fear, panic is somewhere around the corner. Irregular behavior can also stretch widely and markets crash. The future cash flow expectations drop drastically, and this makes people concerned about converting their investment into money rather than future investments. Only when a bear market turns a corner is there rational behavior. It is also important to note that bear markets provide a very large opportunity for investors. It runs in the long-term to get stocks "on sale" at a very low price, which can greatly boost overall returns in the long-term.

Trading Stocks and Order Types

People buy and sell their shares by using a brokerage firm licensed from a broker who helps to make the trade. Going back in time, most stockbrokers were employed only by very rich families and individuals, but over time, there is a range of wide stock brokerages that exists for all prices. For clients that are more budget conscious, reduce brokerage offers a bare-bones service. In some scenario, it is just the sales and executing purchases. Since 20 years ago, trading electronically with the brokerage online gives both opinion and research at a reduced price with a meager asking of $5 or commission.

Paying no attention to the type of brokerage that is used, methods of buying and selling shares is neutral. First of all, the stock quote is gotten. In the early years of the stock exchange, the information concerning the prices was indicated through the **ticker tape**, which is a long ribbon which prints basic data through the telegraph wire and it's the reason we refer to stock quotes as the ticker.

A stock quote has lots of information that includes offers (sometimes referred to as ask) and the current bid prices and the last price that was traded. Bids are the maximum price that someone in the market is ready to pay at a particular time, while an offer is the smallest price that someone is ready to sell at. When you are ready to buy shares, what you will do is to constitute for a bid, and if you are also interested in selling an offer. When the price of an offer and a bid concur, a trade is implemented.

Also, the price information, trading volumes data (that is the number of shares that was traded) is also comprehended. Stock quotes gotten online are sometimes quotes that are real-time which gather second-by-second pieces of information and quote online like the interactive tools, and charts. Quoted stocks are by their ticker symbols which are depicted by capital letters between one and four that sometimes represents the company's name. For instance, the ticker sign for the Apple Inc is AAPL; Caterpillar Inc is CAT and Microsoft Corp is MSFT.

Market and Limit Orders

The type of trade to invest in is to be determined next. A market order is obviously an order that directs the broker (or trading platform online) to sell or buy shares at the best prices available. When you want to buy about 100 shares of AAPL at market, the quote will show: Bid: $139.80 (100), Last: $139.95 (250), offer: $140.00 (50). This explains the last trade was about 250 shares at a price of $139.50 and this points out that at $140.00, 50 shares are being offered and also imagine at $140.00, another 200 are being offered. Market order will then buy at $140.00 shares of 50 and then buy another 50 more when it is at the best price of $140.05.

This market order will not assure us about your expected return, but it does assure us that the amount of shares will be gotten, using the case of 100. When you hear that it's filled, it means that the order has been completed. Sometimes a market order is used in areas where the seller or the buyer is particular about the size of the order that has been filled, and it is not concerned with prices. A limit order states explicitly the price that you are willing to trade.

Limit orders

Limit orders can be designed as all-or-none (AON), which basically means that you might not agree to get shares rather than get all 100 that you desire. If the pioneering limit order in this example is AON, you will not want to buy 50 that you have been given until there is another 50 coming along the way. Limit orders are basically used by those who are concerned with the price they will be getting, but they are not assured by the order size that will be filled. Getting filled vs. prices on the order size are the basic trade-offs between the limit orders and the market.

Stop orders

Stop orders are undetermined on a particular price level that is being attained to put to work. Using a stop order, trades will only be launched when the security you want to sell or buy gets to a specific price (stop price). Once the stock has reached a certain price, stock order necessarily arrives as a market order which is already filled. For example, if you already have a stock ABC which is currently traded at $20 and then you place a stop order and sell at $15, the order will be filled when stocks immediately drop lower than $15, which is already known as a stop-loss order. This assists you in limiting your loss.

This order can be used to assure profits. For example, let's say that you got a stock at $10 per share and then the stock trades presently at $20 per share. When you place a stop order at $15, this gives assurance that the profit is estimated at $5 per share and this depends on how fast the market order will be filled. Stop orders benefits many investors who do not track their stocks for a particular time, and the brokerage might even set the stop orders at no cost.

The weakness of the stop order is that the order is not assured to be filled at the prices in which the investors will have preferred. Once it has been triggered, the stop order turns to a market order which is filled at the best price possible. The price may be reduced more than the price that is given by the stop order. More so, investors must be thorough when it comes to having a stop order; it may be adverse when it is activated by short-term wavering by 15% weekly. A 10% stop-loss set less than the current price might result in the order being initiated at a premature or an inopportune moment.

Other Kinds of Orders

Orders may also be labeled by instruction depending on how long an order is good for, an immediate-or-cancel (IOC) order is not planned, or when it is not executed immediately, this is usually used also with a limit order. When an AOC order is put together with IOC order, it is appointed as fill-or-kill (FOK). A day order is a stop order or limit order that is erased at the end of every trading day and will not be activated until the next day. A good-till-canceled (GTC) order is active when the instruction is given to cancel it, and this might remain active for a few more days.

Margin Trading or Short Selling

In addition to what is described above, margin trading is offered by many brokerages which gives opportunities for customers to borrow cash to buy shares in extras of the amount of money that is in their account. Margin gives room for short selling which is exactly where the participants of the market borrow or share that they do not own, just for them to sell it with the hope of getting them back later in the future at a reduced price. The stock price will go down instead of going up.

Also, using a brokerage, there are fewer ways to get your shares: Direct investment plan (DIPs) and Dividend reinvestment plans (DRIPs). The DIPS individually allows for a reduced cost, allowing shareholders to buy stocks straight from the company. DRIPs are automatically the dividends that are paid by shares, and they are used to buy more of these shares (which include a fraction of shares).

Chapter 7: How to Calculate Stock Market Capitalization and Its Importance

What's That Company's Worth?

The market capitalization for a company's stock is a very important philosophy that is needed for every investor to understand deeply. Though market cap is often discussed on the news every night, and it is also used in business textbooks, you might not be aware of how the market capitalization is being calculated or you might be confused about how it is different from the figures that rise from talks of acquisition and mergers. I will help you change that perspective in this chapter.

Stock Market Capitalization Definition

Putting it in this manner, stock market cap is the considerable total amount of money that it will cost when you get all single shares of a company's stock that has been issued at the current market price.

How to Evaluate Stock Market Capitalization

The formula used in estimating stock market capitalization is just as simple as it may sound, but there is no weird idiosyncrasy, and there are no tricks involved; it is always straightforward.

Stock market capitalization = current stock market price X current share outstanding

Below is a practical example of how to calculate stock market capitalization.

As of July 31, 2018, Coca-Cola company (NYSE: KO) has 4,252,922,000 shares of stock that are outstanding, and each stock is traded at $46. If you are willing to buy all shares of Coca-Cola worldwide, it will cost you 4,252,922,000 x $46= $195,634,412,000 which is more than $195 billion. On Wall Street, individuals will have to refer to $195 billion as Coca Cola's market capitalization.

The Strength and Weakness of Stock Market Capitalization

The stock market cap will allow more investors to get a deep understanding about the company's relative size compared to another, ignoring every particular capital structure. That is the reason why the share of one firm is said to be higher than some other firms. For example, taking Coca-Cola shares of $46 versus Netflix shares of $34, regardless of having an exponentially increased share price, the other has a stock market capitalization of $161 billion which is more than $30 billion less than Coke's. To have a better idea, you can check "How to think about share price" which explains the math of how a stock of $300 is cheaper than that of $10 stock.

On the other hand, stock market cap is also reduced to what exactly it can also say. The greatest disaster of this specific metric is that it does not factor into the fact the company's debt. Let us consider Coca-Cola once more. The company has liabilities of about $27 billion that was used to get the whole business. You will be the one who is responsible for repaying and also servicing which means that Coca-Cola company stock market cap is pegged at $195 billion. It has an enterprise value of $222 billion due to the fact that it is simple and also equal. The other figure is not just what is needed to buy all of the common stock but it is also used to pay off all the debts.

Another great disadvantage of using stock market capitalization as an agent for a company's accomplishment, it does not factor in distributions such as split-offs, dividends, or spin-offs, and they are very important in calculating a notion also known as a Total return. This is very strange to a recent investor, but the total return can help an investor to make more money even when the company goes bankrupt. A significant example is taking a look at the performance of the long-term collapse of the Eastman Kodak. Apart from what was received as dividend over the years, the owners were given the shares of one chemical company at the end of it. Just because the market capitalization went to zero does not mean they lost everything eventually.

Using Market Capitalization to Build a Portfolio

Professional investors also divide their portfolio by the size of their market capitalization. Investors do this because they know that it will allow them to have an advantage since other companies have significantly grown better, but larger companies are more stable, and they have larger dividends.

Here are the types of the breakdown of market capitalization groups that you are going to see being referenced when you start investing. The correct definitions seem to be a bit imprecise, but it is a very good guideline:

- Mega-cap: This is when a company's stock market capitalization is over $100 billion.
- Large-cap: This is when a company's stock market capitalization is within $10 billion to $100 billion.
- Mid-cap: This is when a company's stock market capitalization is within $2 billion to $10 billion.
- Small cap: This is when a company's stock market capitalization is within $250 to $2 billion.
- Micro cap: This is when a company's stock market capitalization is less than $250 million.

Also, be sure to know that you must check the necessary things when using this definition. For example, a person might also refer to a company that has a stock market capitalization of $5 billion as a large cap under certain events.

Chapter 8: Making Money by Investing in Stocks

If you have either listened to the investing press or the financial media, you will have the wrong idea that getting money through buying stocks is a choice of "selecting" the correct stocks, trading very fast, and being used to your computer screen or to the television set, which also includes spending days being intensely preoccupied with what the S & P 500 or Dow Jones Industrial Avenue did currently. This may not be far from the exact truth.

In the real sense, the secrets of getting wealthy from either investing in bonds and buying stocks was added by the father of late Benjamin Graham of investing values when he said "The exact money that will be gotten out of investments will be made just as some of it has been made in the past not just out of purchase and selling but by acquiring securities, receiving dividends and interest and also gains from their value increase for long-term.

Today's investors frequently refer to this Graham's strategy as "holding and buying." To be more precise, investment in common stocks needs more focus on total return and making better decisions to invest in the long-term, it also means that at an outright minimum, you are expected to hold a new post for 5 years knowing full well that you have selected companies that are running well and have a solid finance and they have been known for their management shareholder practices.

For example, choosing four outstanding stocks below to explain how there is an increase in price after five years. High profile investors such as Charlie Munger and Warren Buffet have been holding onto stocks for a period of 25+, even for a longer period of 50+ to make the most of their money. And every other day, many investors have gone in their footsteps, taking a very little amount of money and then investing back in the long-term yields massive wealth. Here are two great examples:

- Retired IRS agent Anne Scheiber built her portfolio of $22 million by investing over $5,000 for more than 50 years.
- Retired secretary Grace Groner built her stock portfolio of $7 million with three $60 shares in 1935.

So many investors still do not get how the process of making money from stocks works and where the wealth starts or even how the process works. We have more resources on advanced topics which are capital gains tax strategies, financial ratio, financial statement analysis, just to name a few, but this is one very important aspect to clear. Just have a cup of coffee with you, be very comfortable while sitting on your reading chair and I'll walk you through a more simplified version of how they can all fit together.

How to Purchase Ownership in a Real Operating Business

When you get shares of stock, you are buying from a portion of that company. Let's imagine that Harrison Fudge Company, a fictional business, has made sales of $10,000,000 and has a net income of $1,000,000. When trying to get funds for growth, the founder of the company got closer to an investment bank that sold stocks to them to the public in an Initial Public Offence or IPO, they might have also said that they do not think that the growth rate is very great and we might have to price this, so that future investment will earn 9% on their investment plus the growth that we can generate which will work to around $11,000,000+ value for the entire company ($11 million divided by $1 million net income= 9% on initial investment returns)." We can assume that the founders decided to sell out completely rather than issue stock to the public.

Underwriters could have said, "You understand that you want to get stocks to sell at $25 per share as it seems very affordable, therefore, we will divide the company into 440,000 pieces of stocks (440,000 x$25= $11,000,000)." This also implies that each "piece" of stock is designated to $2.72 of the profit ($1,000,000 profit divided by 440,000 shares outstanding = $2.72 per share. This figure is also known as Basic EPS (short for earnings per share). In other words, when you get shares from Harrison Fudge Company, you are getting shares directly buying rights to the profits of the pro-rata.

When you acquire 100 shares for $2,500, then you will buy a share of $272 in annual profit in addition to whatever plans (both growth and loss) the company gets. If you think that new management might cause sales to explode, your pro-rata will be 5x greater in a few years, and this will lead to a tremendous attractive investment. How much you make depends on how your capital is allocated.

What makes the situation confusing is that most people do not see the $2.72 profits that are for them. Rather, the Board and management have few options that are left to them which then determine the success of the holdings to a large extent:

1. This can repurchase shares in the open market and destroy it.
2. It can strengthen balance sheets building up the liquid assets or by decreasing the amounts of debts.
3. It can help reinvest funds into future growth by constructing stores, employing new staff, increasing the adverts rate, building more workshops or the number of additional capital expenditures that are needed to increase the profits. Sometimes, this may require you seeking out mergers and acquisitions.
4. It can send you cash dividend for the entire portion or part of the portion; this represents one of the ways to "return capital to shareholders." You can either use the money received to either buy more shares or in any way you deem it fit.

Which option do you feel is ideal for you as the owner? Which option depends solely on the management and what one can earn by reinvesting your cash? If you have a remarkable or flourishing business, think about Wal-Mart or Microsoft in the days where they were just a tiny percentage of what they are currently, which means that paying any cash dividend is going to be a mistake since funds could be reinvested at a very inflated rate. There are times during the first 10 years after the time that Wal-Mart became public, that it earned over 60% on the shareholders equity which is really unbelievable. These kinds of returns typically exists only in fairy tales but not in the real world. Yet, during the time of Sam Walton, the Bentonville-based retailer was able to do it properly and this made him have lots of associates, truck drivers, and outside shareholders that are rich through that process.

Berkshire Hathaway did not pay out any cash dividend while the U.S Bancorp made a firm decision to give back more than 80% of its capital to the shareholders in the form of Stock buybacks and dividends every year. Despite the variations, they both have what it takes to have very high attractive holdings at the correct prices (and if they pay close attention to what is called asset placement) and if they are willing to trade at the exact correct price, for example, a satisfactory dividend-adjusted overvalued.

Any money that you make comes down to a handful of components.

Now that you know this, it is good for you to understand that amassing wealth is a primary function of:

- Dividends: When your earnings are paid to you in the form of a dividend, you can receive money through check in the mail, direct deposit into your brokerage, savings or checking account, or also in the form of additional shares reinvested on your behalf.
- Increase in share price: Long-term, the result of market value is the high profits that are gotten as a result of expansions in the share repurchase or in the business which allows each share great ownership during the time of the business. In other words, if a company with just a $10 stock price increased to 20% for ten years through the collective efforts of share repurchases or expansion, it should be about $620 per share within ten years due to these proceeds, supposing Wall Street keeps to the price-to-earnings ratio equally.

Also, it's possible for you to spend (payout), pile, or donate (give away) these dividends. Not very often, during the time of marked market increase, you might be lucky to have opportunities to make more profits by selling to someone in excess of what the company deserves. In the long-run, the returns are impossible to escape as they are bound to the profits that are being made by the operations in which the business person owns.

Chapter 9: Investing In Preferred Stocks and Things You Should Know

Preferred stocks are mixed between bonds and common stocks. Each of the preferred share stocks is paid normally on an assured dividend which first receives priority (that is the common stockholders will not be able to collect a dividend until the preferred stockholder has been able to pay fully). If the company intends to settle assets when in the proceedings of bankruptcy, preferred stockholders then get paid (if there is any left cash available) before the stockholders, but they will not get it before the bondholders, secured creditors, and creditors.

Often the substantial greater dividend yield for trade-offs collected by preferred stockholders cannot grow the investment as the enterprise becomes bigger. Rather, some provisions are special that will put in a greater influence; preferred stock price is quite sensitive to the interest rate fluctuations and the yields relating to competing investments. This means that capital gains might be enjoyed by the owner who will come from likely buying preferred stocks before the interest rate decrease or increase in credit ranking of the firm, allowing other investors to be ready to accept a lower dividend yield.

Cumulative vs. Non-cumulative Stock

The different meanings of preferred stocks can be distinguished in various forms, even when you are dealing with the same corporation which might issue many preferred stocks "series" as they have been regularly called. This is a necessary feature of preferred stock; the dividend is non-, or it is cumulative. For a cumulative action, the preferred dividend which is not paid are piled into an account; these unpaid dividends are also known as "in arrears." Before dividends can be paid to any common stockholders, the total arrears balance must be given to the preferred stockholders fully.

If the preferred action is non-cumulative, and the payment of the dividend is missed, they (that is the preferred shareholders) will not receive that money again even when the business breaks through months later.

Provisions That Can Influence Preferred Stock Value

There are a number of additional provisions that are affected by the value of preferred stock. Here are few that you should know:

Convertible Preferred stock

The holders of this type of security can convert their preferred stocks into shares of common stocks which gives room for the investors to lock their dividend income and the profit that will be gotten potentially from an increase in the common stock while they are being protected from falling. Under normal conditions, with the appropriate conditions with the correct business, a very smart investor will make lots of money while still enjoying more income and less risk by investing first in the convertible preferred stock.

Voting vs. Non-voting

Preferred stock owners may or do not have the rights to vote; there have been significant cases whereby the owners of the preferred shares only get their voting rights whenever they have not been paid their dividend for a specific period. When you effectively transfer or are not controlling your power to vote to the preferred shareholder, such provisions effectively puts them in positions of the first mortgage bondholder by allowing them their power to collectively emphasize payments on what they claim and permitting their resources. This is consecutively done in some private equity deals, public companies with special financial arrangements, or other situations that are not standard where the lender does not want to pay the higher taxes substantially that could have been owned on interest income where bonds have been issued.

Participating preferred stocks

Often, shares of this kind of preferred stock get a set of dividend including an additional dividend based on a required percentage of either the dividend which is paid to the common shareholders and the net income.

Adjustable rate preferred stocks

The holders of these preferred stocks get a dividend that differentiates them based on a few number of factors required by the business at the issuer's (IPO) initial public offering. The last ten years have witnessed a common trend for all new preferred stocks to have rates dividends floating to reduce the interest rate and explore the possibility to be more viable in the market.

Even with the points listed above, the difference for preferred stock could be completely large; it is possible that an investor comes through a non-voting cumulative participant which converts preferred issues.

How Changes in the Common Stock Prices Influences Preferred Stock

For example, if a very big pharmaceutical company reveals a new cure for the common cold, the common stock for the company will increase so much in anticipation of billions of dollars in ten places in which the shareholders will expect more from the company in the near future. At a given period, the company's preferred shares will not move more in price except that the extent to which the preferred dividend is now better due to more earnings: a series of events that could lead to change in the market value of the preferred rising and falling yields. In spite of it, the preferred shareholders will have missed out on the big capital gains, although also collecting the dividend checks.

Weeks later, the company then announced that the cure has not been effective. The common stock price fall drastically; will the preferred stock of the company also fall? So far, the company is still making the preferred stock dividend payments and price to remain very stable. However, if the investor owns a convertible preferred share ('PERCS" which means Preference Equity Redemption Cumulative Stock). In this case, PERCS price would drastically increase or decrease depending solely on what the investor could realize by converting the shares into common stocks. If the holder does not convert his shares or get more preferred shares at an increased price, he will not experience loss of capital.

Who Should Invest In Preferred Stocks?

In different methods, insulated preferred stocks seem very attractive, but the truth lies in the preferred stock. Speaking generally, it will not make sense for individual investors. From another point of view, preferred stocks investment can be a very profitable economic venture for corporate portfolios, why? Federal tax laws require paying 30% of their income tax preferred dividends which mean that a full 70% is free of tax. This exclusion is not given to individual investors. Your portfolio will surely have an increase after tax-yield when you invest in corporate bonds when the rates are pleasing or municipal bonds when you have an increased tax bracket (that is to know if it offers an increased tax yield, you will need to calculate what is called the taxable equivalent yield).

Also, it is important that as a bond investor, you might likely get a senior claim in investments as opposed to the lower class position given by many of the preferred stocks. Note the words of the legendary investor, Benjamin Graham, who said that it is almost mistaken to allow an investor to purchase a preferred stock issued at a close value as it experience that shows with patience the opportunity will arise to have it at a substantially reduced value that will later increase in value.

Chapter 10: Tips for Investing in Stock Market

In preceding chapters of this book, an extensive discussion has been made on the basics of stock market investing, its benefits also highlighted. It is time for you to take action by investing in the profitable business of stock market. As a beginner, you will need these tips to get a great start to your stock market investment career.

1. Set Long-Term Goals

If goals are not fixed, your stock market investment won't have any meaning. Ask yourself these few questions: Why do you choose stock market investment? When do you need your capital back, six months, a year, or longer? Are you saving for education expenses, for a future business, or retirement?

You should set your goal for investing, and the likely time you may need the funds in the future. If you are planning to spend your investment on some project within a few years, consider investing somewhere else; the stock market is volatile and does not assure that all your capital will be available when needed.

When you know the amount of capital needed and when it's needed in the future, you can calculate the amount to invest, and the return on investment (ROI) required to achieve the needed result. You can make use of the free fiscal calculators online to estimate the amount of capital needed for your education expenses, future business, retirement, or other plans.

Note that your portfolio growth depends upon three mutually dependent factors:

- The invested capital
- The annual net income on your capital
- The length in years of your venture

Start saving massively today to receive the highest possible return based on your risk threshold.

2. Understand Your Risk Tolerance

Everyone has a specific risk tolerance threshold that is genetically based. Our education level, income, and wealth affect the risk tolerance positively while an increase in age affects risk tolerance negatively.

Your risk tolerance is the way you react to risk and how anxious you feel with the presence of risk. Risk tolerance is explained as "the rate at which a person decides to risk being subjected to a less favorable outcome in the quest for a more favorable outcome." Conversely, would you forego parting with $100 to earn $1,000?

The perception one has towards risk affects one's risk tolerance. For example, in the early 1900s, one would have perceived it as very risky to fly in an airplane, but today people view it as less risky as most people fly and travel by air. Equally, most people today would see riding a horse as a significant risk because few people ride horse nowadays.

So also, in investing, the idea of perception is important. As more knowledge is acquired on stock (as this book has provided so far), you may begin to perceive investing in stock as less risky.

By having a good grasp of your risk forbearance, investments that tends to make you feel anxious will be avoided. As a beginner, the rule of thumb in stock market investing is never to own an asset that prevents you from sleeping at night.

3. Control Your Emotions

The inability to put one's emotion in check is one of the biggest obstacles in stock market profitability. In the short-term, the company's stock prices reflect the entire investment community combined emotions. The price of stock could possibly decline when most investors become worried about a business and when most investors feel its stock price is projected to appreciate.

As discussed in chapter six about the bear and bull, people who feel pessimistic about the stock market is called a "bear," while those who feel positive are called a "bull." In the stock exchange market, the constant struggle between the bears and bulls is revealed in the ever-changing price of shares. Speculations and rumors drive these short-term movements.

Tension and insecurity are often heightened when stock prices move against our expectations. Should I sell my stock to cut losses? Should I keep hold of the stock in the hope that the price will recover? Should I purchase more?

Several questions may come to your mind in the course of stock market trading. However, avoid taking emotion led decisions; focus on the facts and not feelings. If you decide not to put funds into a specific stock, you should have a sincere reason for this and the consequences you will face if you do.

4. Handle Basics First

Before investing in stock, acquire more knowledge about the stock market basics and the individual securities component of the market. Except you are investing in the exchange-traded fund (ETF), your attention will be based on individual securities, rather than the whole market. There are certain times when every stock gravitates towards the same direction; even at less than an average of 100 points, the company's shares will increase in price.

The aspects you should gather more knowledge about before you make your first purchase include:

• Understand the meanings of metrics like P/E ratio, return on equity (ROE), earnings per share (EPS), and compound annual growth rate (CAGR). Knowing how they are calculated and being able to compare different companies with these metrics is vital.

• You should understand the performance and differences of "fundamental" and "technical" analysis.

• Understand the different stock market order type and how they affect stock market price.

• Understand the different types of investment accounts, its regulations, and requirements.

-

5. Diversify Your Investments

Diversifying your investment is a popular way to manage risk. Wise investors own shares in different companies, industries, and sometimes in different countries. This is to forestall any bad event from affecting all the investments in one swoop.

6. Avoid Leverage

Leverage in simple terms means lending funds to invest in stock market. Banks and brokerage firms can provide a loan to purchase stocks, usually 50% of the purchase value. Making use of borrowed money for stock market investment "levers" or exaggerates the price movement. For instance, if the stock increases to $200 per share and you sell it. If you had not borrowed any money to fund your investment, your return would be 100% on your investment [($20,000 -$10,000)/$10,000]. However, if you had borrowed $5,000 to buy the share and sold at $200 per share, you would earn 300% returns [(20,000-$5,000)/$5,000] after repaying the $5,000 loan and excluding the interest the broker receives.

This sounds great with an increasing stock price, but when you consider the other scenario where the stock price depreciates and falls to $50 per share rather than $200, you will experience a 100% loss of your initial investment, including the interest cost to the broker [($5,000-$5,000)/$5,000].

Leverage is a double-edged knife, and it is a tool best used for an expert in stock market investing. Therefore, minimize your risk as a new entrant into the stock market to ensure long-term profitability.

Carefully studying and adhering to these tips will set you on a pedestal to success in the stock market as a beginner.

Conclusion

Historically, investment in the stock market has enjoyed an increased advantage and upsurge over other investment types. It has shown total visibility, easy liquidity, and possesses an active regulation which gives room for a level playing field for all investors.

Stock market investing has proven to be an excellent opportunity to acquire immense asset value for those willing to cultivate a lifestyle of saving. As a beginner ready to delve into the broad market of stock, ensure you have read all the chapters in this book meticulously to acquire knowledge and soon you will also gain experience to properly manage risk and make a long-term profit from your investment. The earlier you start your stock market investment, the better for you as it's a long-term investment.

Lastly, learn to take each step at a time; don't try to jump several steps on the journey to profitability in stock market investment. Walk before you begin to run! I wish you the best investment decision, and I hope to be a part of your success story.

Don't miss out!

Visit the website below and you can sign up to receive emails whenever Gary Jenks publishes a new book. There's no charge and no obligation.

https://books2read.com/r/B-A-AYPH-HDGAB

BOOKS 2 READ

Connecting independent readers to independent writers.